Wild Animals OF Africa

Story and photographs by
Beatrice Brown Borden

Random House  New York

Copyright © 1982 by Beatrice Brown Borden. All rights reserved under International and Pan-American Copyright Conventions. Published in the United States by Random House, Inc., New York, and simultaneously in Canada by Random House of Canada Limited, Toronto.

Library of Congress Cataloging in Publication Data: Borden, Beatrice Brown. Wild animals of Africa. SUMMARY: Follows a day in the lives of animals and birds that inhabit the African grasslands. 1. Zoology—Africa—Juvenile literature. [1. Grassland animals. 2. Animals. 3. Africa] I. Title. QL336.B66 599.096 AACR2 82-5262 ISBN: 0-394-85306-7 (trade); 0-394-95306-1 (lib. bdg.) Manufactured in the United States of America 1 2 3 4 5 6 7 8 9 0

Photographs on pages 11, 16 (top),
and back cover by Edie Ker

It is early morning in far-off Africa. The mother lionesses are very tired. They were out all night hunting for food for the whole family. Now they are stretched out and ready to sleep in the warmth of the morning sun.

The little cub spent the night resting in a safe, grassy hideout. So he is wide awake and ready to play.

His mother and aunts wish that the pesky little cub would let them sleep. But he has other ideas!

The big, handsome male
lion can't be bothered
with any of this. He
looks on, quite bored.

The little cub's
games are getting
to be rough and
rowdy.

Finally his mother gets
up and leads him away
from the sleepy lionesses.

These wildebeests have huddled together
all night. Now, in the morning light,
they start to walk around, eating the
grass around them.

Because there is no place to hide on
the grassy plains where they live,
they must stay close to each other,
protecting themselves from animals
hunting for a meal.

Although wildebeests look like bearded
cows, they are not. They are a kind
of African antelope.

Antelopes come in many shapes and sizes.

This topi is a big one, weighing 290 pounds.

These impalas are antelopes, too, but they are smaller than the topi. The male is called a ram. He has long, curved, sharp horns, which he uses to protect his family.

There are thousands of little Thompson gazelles in the African grasslands. They are no bigger than goats. Both the male and the female have horns and tiny black tails, which they wag a lot.

There are few dik-diks like this one on the plains. They are dainty antelopes, only one foot tall. But they have big eyes and ears.

The largest African antelope is the eland. A male eland can weigh as much as a car! You can recognize him by his corkscrew horns.

Can you guess why these beautiful birds are called crowned cranes?

Cape buffalo are always ready for a fight. So most animals stay clear of their big wide horns.

There are thousands of little Thompson gazelles in the African grasslands. They are no bigger than goats. Both the male and the female have horns and tiny black tails, which they wag a lot.

There are few dik-diks like this one on the plains. They are dainty antelopes, only one foot tall. But they have big eyes and ears.

The largest African antelope is the eland. A male eland can weigh as much as a car! You can recognize him by his corkscrew horns.

Can you guess why these beautiful birds are called crowned cranes?

Cape buffalo are always ready for a fight. So most animals stay clear of their big wide horns.

As the sun gets higher in the sky, the grasslands get warmer and the animals get thirsty. This cheetah mother has brought her cubs to a water hole for a drink.

Her beautiful spotted fur helps her to blend into the land. So she is hard to see as she stalks the prairie looking for a meal. For short runs, she is the fastest runner on earth.

Another spotted animal is the leopard.
After dark he will begin to look for
a meat dinner. Because he is not as
fast as the cheetah, he has to sneak
up on his prey.

When he has finished eating, small
animals called scavengers will move
in to clean up.

This baby hyena is watching his mother as she leaves their den to find food.

Hyenas are scavengers. They will eat up what is left of a leopard's or a lion's meal. But if there are no scraps around, they will catch their own dinner.

These maribou storks are part-time scavengers.
They eat leftovers but also hunt rats and
snakes on their own.

The silver-backed jackal
is a scavenger through
and through. He is a
clever fellow, who is
always waiting around
for some scraps.

Scavengers help to keep
the prairie clean and
stop the spread of diseases.

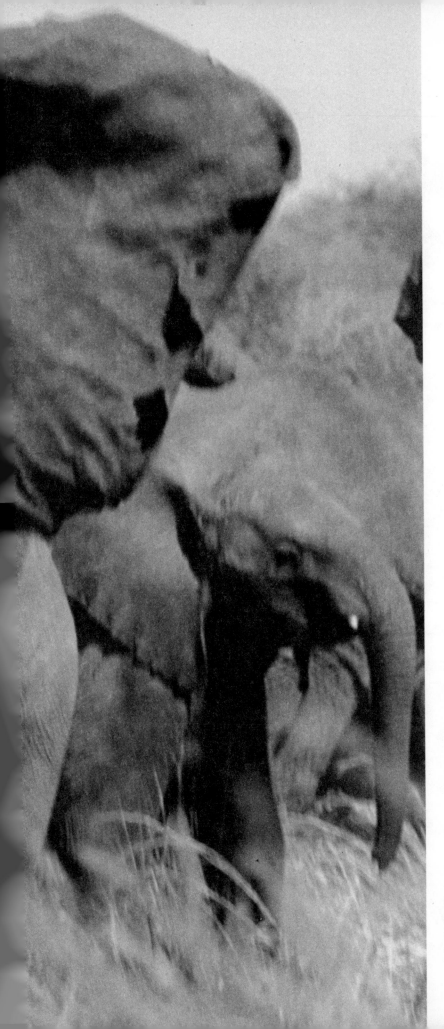

Some animals eat no meat. The little bronze sunbird drinks the sweet nectar in flowers.

African elephants eat grasses, leaves, tree bark, and fruits. They are the biggest animals on land. Their ears are so large, they can easily hear far-off sounds.

When an elephant spots an enemy, it will spread its huge ears and flap them back and forth as a warning. It may also attack, making a lot of loud noise as it charges its enemy.

An elephant's trunk is very strong. It can tear a whole branch off a tree. But it can pick up a tiny berry, too. A trunk is also good for drinking water, smelling danger, and guiding babies.

The wrinkled skin of this old elephant looks tough. But it is really very sensitive. To keep it cool and insect free, the elephant picks up earth with his trunk and blows it onto his back.

Cattle egrets eat the insects that do land on elephants. So the egrets are welcome guests.

As the day gets hotter, the elephants spend more time in the water. They lie down and roll in the muck. This is another way to protect their skin from the hot sun and biting insects.

The secretary bird is as tall as a baby elephant. The long, thin feathers that run down his neck make him an amazing sight as he struts around looking for eggs, rats, snakes, and lizards.

These elephants are feeling very hot in the afternoon sun. Can you guess where they are headed? To water, of course!

No, these are not red elephants. They are gray African elephants like the ones in the other pictures. They just look red!

They live in a place where the soil is red. When they roll in the wet, red muck of their watering pond, their whole bodies get covered with red clay.

While his mother is resting, the playful cub is still looking for a game. He hopes the jaçana bird will want to play.

To keep cool, this lioness has climbed into the shady branches of a tall tree. Maybe she will feel a little breeze up there.

The leopard, too, is trying to keep cool, high up in a sausage tree. He naps for a while but tries to keep one eye open. Maybe a good meal will come by beneath the tree.

The African rhinoceros is a big, scary-looking
animal. His skin is so tough that he can spend
hours lying in the hot sun. Baby rhinos have skin
that is much more tender. In the hot afternoon,
a mother will lead her calf to some mud. He will
roll around in it and come out dirty but cool.

If a calf is in danger, a mother rhino will charge and attack. It's no fun to tangle with the sharp rhinoceros horn!

These ostriches are the largest birds in the world—and the fastest. Even a cheetah cannot catch one in a long race. So an ostrich doesn't need to fly. And in fact it can't fly. It is too big to get off the ground.

The big, clumsy hippopotamus looks mean, but she is a gentle water cow. In the early morning she travels from her river home to grasslands ashore. There she finds food for herself and her calf. Then the two return to the water to stay cool and to play with the other hippos.

If a calf is in danger, a mother rhino will charge and attack. It's no fun to tangle with the sharp rhinoceros horn!

These ostriches are the largest birds in the world—and the fastest. Even a cheetah cannot catch one in a long race. So an ostrich doesn't need to fly. And in fact it can't fly. It is too big to get off the ground.

The big, clumsy hippopotamus looks mean, but she is a gentle water cow. In the early morning she travels from her river home to grasslands ashore. There she finds food for herself and her calf. Then the two return to the water to stay cool and to play with the other hippos.

Millions of years ago, when dinosaurs were on earth, there were pelicans like these. Today many thousands of them live in the lakes of East Africa.

Hippos spend most of the long, hot day in the cool river water. They can stay underwater for four minutes—or more!

A crocodile can stay
underwater for more
than an hour!

The croc is one of the
ugliest animals alive.
And he's just as mean.
He will attack and eat
any animal that crosses
his path—either on
land or in the water.

This is not a mother bird with babies. It is a group of full-grown flamingos. The tall one is called a greater flamingo. The smaller ones are lesser flamingos. These beautiful pink birds live happily together on shallow African lakes.

Zebras look like small, chunky horses with black and white stripes. No two zebras have the same stripe pattern!

Big herds of zebras travel together to any place that has water. But they don't go near the water holes except when lions are likely to be asleep. Even then, at least one zebra keeps his head up, watching for danger.

Young zebras are called foals. They have brown stripes that turn black when they grow up. Until then, foals stay close to their mothers—and the rest of the herd. In order to keep up, they must learn to run almost as soon as they are born.

The masked weaver bird builds its nest upside down in an acacia tree. The little bird sees many giraffes that stop by to munch on the acacia leaves.

The giraffe is the tallest animal in the world. Because he can be 18 feet tall and has very sharp eyes, he can see danger a long way off.

A giraffe's legs are six feet long, and his feet are the size of dinner plates. He uses them to give good, hard kicks. So lions usually keep away from giraffes.

All giraffes live in grassy woodlands. So they have plenty of bushes and trees to nibble on. They need little water and get most of it from eating juicy acacia leaves. The giraffes' tough, hairy lips protect against the acacia's sharp thorns. Their long tongues reach carefully between the thorns to get to the leaves.

The ground hornbill has long black eyelashes that stand out against its bright red face and throat. Late in the afternoon, when the lions wake up, the hornbill grunts a warning. The warthog family hears the hornbill's cry. Lots of little warthog tails stick up in the air as they run to safety.

Late in the afternoon, the
sun starts to sink and the
air cools off. Now the
lioness is ready to leave
her shady resting place.
She tells her little cub
to climb down, too, and
she watches carefully as
he feels his way down
the tree.

The lioness's sharp eyes look all around her. It is hunting time again.

A young lion at the watering hole can feel the excitement of the hunt in the air.

The little cub is too young to hunt, so he is put in a bushy hiding place to wait for his mother. It has been a long, hot day. He has played a lot. It is dark now, and cool. He is very, very tired.